Snow

;

*Only a hill; but all of life to me,
up there, between the sunset and the sea.*

GEOFFREY WINTHROP YOUNG, MOUNTAINEER & POET (1876 – 1958)

Snowdonia's
best
Mountain Walks

Carl Rogers

MARA BOOKS

www.marabooks.co.uk
www.northerneyebooks.com

First published in February 2008 by **Mara Books**,
22 Crosland Terrace, Helsby, Frodsham, Cheshire WA6 9LY.

Telephone: 01928 723744

Second edition May, 2010

ISBN 978 1 902512 19 8

Advice to readers and users of this guide

Whilst every effort has been made to ensure that the information in this book is correct, the author or the publisher can accept no responsibility for errors, loss or injury however caused. Check all details before you proceed. Your use of this book indicates your assumption of the risks involved in mountain walking and scrambling and is an acknowledgement of your own sole responsibility for your safety.

Graphic design, photography and maps by Carl Rogers
© Carl Rogers 2010

British Library Cataloguing-in-publication data.
A catalogue is available for this book from the British Library.

Maps based on out of copyright Ordnance Survey mapping

Contents

Introduction

SNOWDONIA IS ONE OF THE MOST CELEBRATED AND SPECTACULAR mountain areas in Britain and its tallest summit—Snowdon—stands higher than any mountain south of the Scottish Highlands in either England, Ireland or Wales.

The area covered by the National Park includes most of the ancient land of 'Snowdon'—a Saxon name meaning 'snowy downs' or 'hills of snow'—and embraces all the highland between Afon Conwy in the north and the Dyfi estuary on its southern fringe. Its western boundary is defined by the coastal lands of Cardigan Bay between Harlech and Aberdyfi, and it reaches east to include the town of Bala and its famous lake. In Welsh it is known as 'Eryri', an ancient name of uncertain translation but thought to mean either 'the highland' or 'abode of eagles'.

The hills and mountains of Snowdonia will captivate any lover of wild mountain scenery, with around 100 summits above 610 metres/2,000 feet and fourteen which exceed 914 metres—the elite 3,000-foot mountains. Of these, four raise their summits above 1,000 metres.

The peaks of the Snowdon Horseshoe seen from Llynnau Mymbyr, Capel Curig

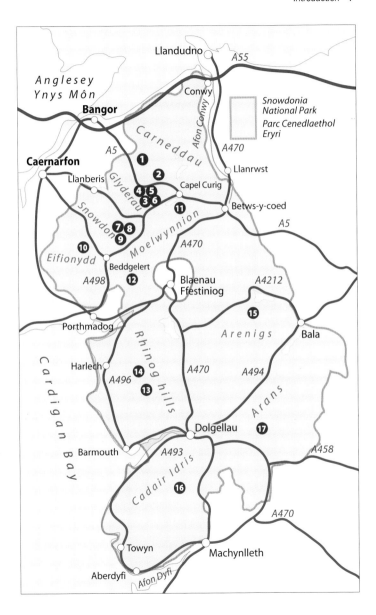

The highest, most rugged and most distinctive mountains are all located in the north around Snowdon, where you will find celebrities like the rock peak of Tryfan and the knife-edge ridge of Crib Goch. But there is also the lesser known Carneddau, a high plateauland of broad pillowy summits containing the largest area of land above 2,500 feet in the whole of Wales.

Snowdon and the Glyderau are undoubtedly the best known hill groups and are similar in character, with acres of fine rock scenery, narrow ridges and pointed Alpine-like summits. This is the place for drama, with superb scrambles like the famous Snowdon Horseshoe; the North Ridge of Tryfan; Bristly Ridge and Y Gribin on Glyder Fach. Be prepared to share these delights though, Snowdon is the most visited summit in Britain, attracting over half a million visitors a year and the summit of Tryfan is rarely a place of solitude.

Similar in character and also well known is Cadair Idris. Like Snowdon, Cadair is a complex, bulky and rugged mountain—a group

The dramatic skyline of Tryfan's East Face seen across the shoulder of Gallt yr Ogof

The striking summit of Cnicht seen from the marshlands of Afon Glaslyn

of summits connected by ridges and separated by deep glacial cwms. There are probably more routes to its summit than any other peak in Snowdonia with the exception of Snowdon itself.

To the west and south of Snowdon the lower hills of Eifionydd and the Moelwynion are dominated by their giant neighbour, but the Eifionydd hills offer fine ridge walking with the famous Nantlle Ridge providing one of the best walks of its kind in Wales.

The Moelwynion is a large area of wild moors and distinctive medium-height summits, the most famous being Cnicht ('knight')—sometimes known as the 'Welsh Matterhorn' on account of its fine central ridge and pointed summit when seen from the old marshlands of Afon Glaslyn. Industrial ruination associated with the Blaenau Ffestiniog slate quarries scars the southern slopes of the group, but thankfully has little impact on the upper mountainsides—a rolling plateau of sparkling lakes with grand views of the higher tops and out across Cardigan Bay.

Between Snowdon and Cadair Idris is a large area—almost half the National Park—of lower hills and moors which are largely unknown.

The western half of this area is occupied by some of Snowdonia's most remarkable hills, the Rhinogydd. They line the coastal land of Ardudwy between the estuaries of Afon Dwyryd and Afon Mawddach and form a striking skyline when seen from either the coast or the wild moors to the east. What they lack in height they make up for in ruggedness—not the towering near-vertical cliffs of Snowdon and Tryfan, but strange horizontal terraces and twisted layering. There is nothing like it in the rest of Wales and away from the famous 'Roman Steps' you are likely to have the hills to yourself.

To the east, beyond the A470, lies a large area of wild moors and isolated hills—possibly the least visited in Snowdonia. If you enjoy a feeling of remoteness and like to have the mountains to yourself the Arenig is the place for you, but be prepared for some trackless walking over bogs and through the occasional conifer plantation.

Finally we come to the Aran ridge, tucked away and almost forgotten in southeast Snowdonia. Although a little higher than Cadair Idris, the Arans are generally overlooked in favour of their more rugged and more famous neighbour, but this is a fine mountain group containing the highest summit south of Snowdon.

The walks and scrambles

This guide gathers together what are—in the author's opinion at least—the best of Snowdonia's numerous mountain walks and scrambles in each of the main hill groups. This means that the walks are spread throughout the National Park and not just concentrated on the 'honeypot' areas around Snowdon itself. As a result there is at least one walk in each of its nine main hill groups.

A note of caution—although each walk carries a detailed route description, I have assumed that anyone following the routes will have the ability to navigate independently of the book using a large scale Ordnance Survey map and compass. (The 1:25,000 Explorer maps sheet numbers L17, OL18 and OL32 cover all the walks in the book.) It is important to remember that this is not an optional skill, it is a basic requirement and without it you are not safe to either walk or scramble in the mountain environment. This guide will not help you if you become lost on the mountains, particularly in bad weather or poor visibility.

It should also be noted that all the routes are intended as summer walks or scrambles in fine, dry conditions. Poor visibility, wind, rain and especially winter conditions with ice and snow, turn the mountains into a very different environment. If you do venture onto the hills in these conditions, be sure you are equipped and experienced enough to deal with them. For winter walking conditions in snow and ice, an ice axe and the knowledge of how to use it to arrest a slide is a minimum requirement. Suitable clothing is just as essential.

On the routes labelled **SCRAMBLE** you will need to be confident climbing rocks which, although not technically difficult (not graded rock climbs), will still require agility, a steady head and could well be in an exposed position where a fall would be serious. Having said that, all the scrambles described are generally completed without the use of ropes and specialist equipment in normal conditions, ie. dry, summer weather with good visibility and free from snow and ice. If you are in any doubt about the above, avoid these routes. All the scrambles become winter climbs under ice and snow and are beyond the scope of this guide.

Aran Benllyn and Aran Fawddwy from Bala Lake (Llyn Tegid)

Carnedd Dafydd and the prominent nose of the Llech Ddu Spur

1. Cwm Llafar Horseshoe

Outline: **SCRAMBLE** *A long but gentle walk into a spectacular mountain cwm is followed by easy scrambling with a little exposure on a fine shattered arête in a superb setting. Once on the high summit plateau, easy walking around the rim of Cwm Llafar above the impressive Black Ladders leads to Carnedd Llewelyn and Yr Elen. Descent is by the rocky northeast ridge of Yr Elen into Cwm Caseg.*

Distance: *17km/10½ miles.*

Height gained: *1,200/3,900ft.*

Summits: *Carnedd Dafydd, Carnedd Llewelyn & Yr Elen.*

Starting point: *Gerlan in upper Bethesda (Grid ref: SH 633 663). There is very limited parking in Gerlan, official parking is available off High Street (A5) in the centre of Bethesda, with a walk up to Gerlan to start (Grid ref: SH 625 664).*

THE DARK DRIPPING PRECIPICE known as the 'Black Ladders' (Ysgolion Duon) has a fearsome reputation for its hard, exposed winter climbs, but yields few quality rock climbs due to the amount of drainage taken by the face. This produces wet slimy rock and accounts for the dark black colour from which the precipice takes its name. The main face is a spectacular near vertical wall some 250 metres high and almost 1km/½mile wide. Only at its western edge is there any suitable weakness to tempt the scrambler were a shattered nose-like arête (Llech Ddu Spur) protrudes from the main face. The lower section of the ridge is definitely off-limits to the scrambler, but a detour into the cwm to the right allows access to the middle and upper sections of the ridge which provide the best scrambling.

The Llech Ddu Spur is a superb route onto the high tops of the Carneddau and sadly almost the only scramble of its kind in the entire group. It is of a similar standard to the North Ridge of Tryfan or the rock ridge of Y Gribin. By the described route the scrambling is straightforward and there is surprisingly little exposure, although care in finding the correct route is required. Not recommended in poor visibility or under winter conditions. *(The scramble section of the route can be avoided by ascending the northwest ridge of Carnedd Dafydd—see map below.)*

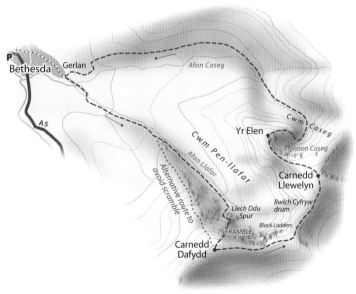

The route: To reach Gerlan from Bethesda, turn right out of the car park along 'High Street', then go left into 'Allt Pen y Bryn' (just before the Spar shop). Keep right at a fork—'Pant-glas Road'—and ahead at the next two crossroads eventually following 'Ffordd Gerlan'.

Follow 'Ffordd Gerlan' out of Gerlan leaving the houses behind and continue along lane for almost 1km/½mile. Immediately after the road curves right over the river for the second time, bear left along a 'Private Road'. In a few yards and before the waterworks, bear right over a stile beside a gate. Go ahead up the field edge to a ladder stile in the top left corner. Turn left over the stile then right onto a path which shortly passes to the right of ruins. The path is well defined now and soon you are walking with the shapely cone of Yr Elen ahead. Immediately after a footbridge the path forks—keep right as signed and soon cross a wall by means of a ladder stile.

Keep ahead through a large field aiming approximately for the gap between Carnedd Dafydd and Yr Elen to the final stile before the open mountain pastures. The path is better defined now and in about 200m, just before a small square enclosure with iron railings, splits (to avoid the Llech Ddu Spur scramble, bear right up Carnedd Dafydd's northwest ridge at this point). Keep ahead on the well-defined footpath beside Afon Llafar and walk almost to the head of the valley below the towering cliffs of the 'Black Ladders'.

One of the pinnacles on the Llech Du Spur with Yr Elen behind

Yr Elen and the northeast ridge seen from Carnedd Llewelyn

To the right of the main cliff there is a large triangular buttress which forms the base of the Llech Ddu Spur. This is a classic example of a 'truncated spur', created by a glacier cutting off a ridge or spur which would previously have protruded into the valley. For the scrambler a direct line is impossible, but a detour to the right allows access to the upper ridge which gives pleasant scrambling onto the summit slopes of Carnedd Dafydd.

Head towards the right-hand end of the triangular buttress where a black stain from a small cascade can be seen. Immediately to the left of the cascade a narrow path zig-zags steeply up scree into the cwm above. Continue steeply and directly up to a point almost level with the base of the large crag to the right which is split by a prominent gully or chimney. The faint path now turns left across a shattered grassy terrace to a small grass platform on the skyline by white quartz rocks. This is the start of the scrambling.

Scramble up the broken wall directly above. The exact line can be varied at will but remains at a similar standard. Higher up the ridge levels and a short easy section with small pinnacles follows (photo on page 14).

The angle steepens again and pleasant easy scrambling with little exposure continues until the ridge eventually merges into the upper shattered slopes of the mountain. Continue up to arrive a little to the east of the summit.

From Carnedd Dafydd head east along the broad, easy, almost level ridge with superb views right into the northern cwms of the Glyderau and left into the gulf of Cwm Pen-llafar where you will get good views back to the Llech Ddu Spur. The ridge soon swings north over Bwlch Cyfryw-drum where a short rise leads to the highest point in the range—Carnedd Llewelyn—just 21m lower than Snowdon.

From Carnedd Llewelyn take the path which strikes out west across the plateau. Soon you have a view of Yr Elen's impressive northeast face rising above the hidden Cwm Caseg. The connecting ridge looks quite striking but sadly provides little scrambling.

From Yr Elen the most interesting descent is by the northeast ridge which falls directly from the summit—a mixture of shattered spiky rocks separated by grass. The main interest is in the upper section where you will need your hands here and there. Once the scree to your right is replaced by grass break away from the crest and descend to the tiny lake—Ffynnon Caseg—in its remote hidden cwm.

From the outflow of the lake descend just to the right of the stream, gradually moving further to the right to avoid boggy ground as you descend. As the valley flattens a path establishes itself at the point where the drier slopes to the right meet the boggy, waterlogged ground of the valley base. Where the valley opens out, follow the narrow but visible path which takes a contouring line above the waterlogged valley floor ahead, following the line of a now dried out but still visible leat.

Follow the path for about 1.5km/¾mile before looking for a faint path which drops diagonally-left to a group of well-built sheep pens which can be seen below. Join a farm track by the sheep pens and follow this for another 2km/1 mile until you reach a small building on the left. Turn left here down a wall-enclosed track which leads into a lane by cottages. Follow the lane back to Gerlan.

Carnedd Llewelyn seen from the south across the Ogwen Valley

2. *The southern Carneddau from Llyn Ogwen*

Outline: *A steady ascent and a short easy scramble to Pen-yr Ole Wen is followed by an elevated ridge walk over three high summits with wide views south to the Glyderau and Tryfan. Descent is by Carnedd Llewelyn's long southeast ridge, across the narrow Bwlch Eryl Farchog to Pen yr Helgi Du and then by the gentle ridge of Y Braich.*

Distance: *19km/11/¾ miles (longest option).*

Height gained: 1,400m/4,410ft.

Summits: *Pen-yr Ole Wen, Carnedd Dafydd, Carnedd Llewelyn, Yr Elen & Pen yr Helgi Du.*

Starting point: *There is ample free parking at the eastern end of Llyn Ogwen between Glan Dena and Gwern Gof Uchaf. Grid ref: SH 668 606.*

THE MOST POPULAR ACCESS TO THE HIGH TOPS of the Carneddau is from the Ogwen valley to the south which avoids the long approach walks required from the north, east and west. This route is excellent in either a clockwise or anticlockwise direction and once the climbing is done, you can cruise along the fine elevated ridge between Carnedd Dafydd and Carnedd Llewelyn with minimal effort. Views are superb, particularly south to Tryfan, the Glyderau and Cwm Idwal.

If you need to shorten the walk, this can be done at Bwlch Eryl Farchog by taking the path down to Ffynnon Llugwy and then following the reservoir access road down to the A5. You can also leave out Yr Elen.

The route: From the A5 at the eastern end of Llyn Ogwen, cross the bridge and follow the track past 'Glan Dena' towards 'Tal y Llyn Ogwen' farm. Immediately before the farm, turn right up to cross a stile in the wall on the left. After the stile, the path curves right to follow the eastern bank of Afon Lloer. Cross the stream higher up and follow it until the angles eases as you approach Cwm Lloer.

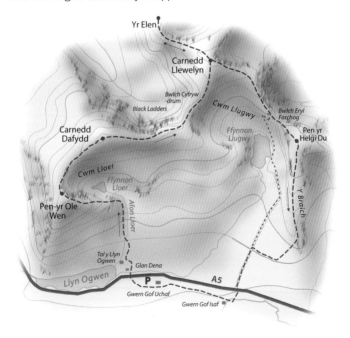

On the ridge between Pen-yr Ole Wen and Carnedd Dafydd

Head left before you reach the lake to begin the ascent of Pen-yr Ole Wen's east ridge. A broken rock spur is negotiated by a short easy gully scramble to gain a well-defined path which keeps close to the crags overlooking the south wall of the Cwm Lloer.

Pen-yr Ole Wen is the perfect viewpoint for the magnificent hollow of Cwm Idwal enclosed by Glyder Fawr and Y Garn and is well worth the short detour to the top of the southwest ridge.

From Pen-yr Ole Wen a good path heads northeast along the ridge to Carnedd Dafydd (about 2km/1 mile away), then above the huge cliffs known as the 'Black Ladders' (Ysgolion Duon). A short drop to Bwlch Cyfryw-drum is followed by a steady ascent over scree to Carnedd Llewelyn, Snowdonia's third highest mountain and the highest point in the Carneddau.

If you want to include the summit of Yr Elen it is a straightforward 3km/1½ mile out-and-back detour along the northwest ridge.

From Carnedd Llewelyn follow the broad east ridge with the deep glacial trough of Cwm Eigiau ahead. The ridge is steep at first, then more gentle and grassy until you reach the rim of the massive Craig yr Ysfa and its famous 'Amphitheatre'. The ridge narrows now and there is a little scrambling to reach Bwlch Eryl Farchog. (You could shorten the walk here if needed by taking the path which heads right down to the lake and follow the reservoir road down to the A5.) A short scramble beyond the bwlch leads to Pen yr Helgi Du, another superb viewpoint particularly for Tryfan seen dramatically across the valley.

From Here head due south along the gentle, rounded ridge of Y Braich. Almost at the bottom of the ridge pass through a gap in a crossing wall and bear right over open ground to cross a leat by a footbridge. This feeds water into the nearby Llyn Cowlyd Reservoir. Turn right now and follow the leat to the reservoir access road leading to up Ffynnon Llugwy. Turn left down the road to the A5.

To avoid the 2km/1 mile or so back along the A5, turn left and just before a small conifer wood go right over the stile and make your way through a boulder-strewn field to a group of old pines. The stile here leads onto a bridleway, once the main road through the valley. Turn right and follow the path back to Gwern Gof Uchaf farm to reach the A5.

Following the east ridge of Carnedd Dafydd above the Black Ladders

Llyn Bochlwyd

3. Glyder Fach & Glyder Fawr from Llyn Ogwen

Outline: *A good footpath takes you via the high mountain hollow of Cwm Bochlwyd to Bwlch Tryfan and up onto the Glyder plateau by the mountain's rounded eastern shoulder. Almost level walking across the plateau between the two summits gives superb views and allows the walker to enjoy the unusual rock architecture. Descent is by the famous Devil's Kitchen and Cwm Idwal where the fine rock scenery continues.*

Distance: *9.75km/6 miles.*

Height gained: *860m/2,820ft.*

Summits: *Glyder Fach & Glyder Fawr.*

Starting point: *Parking is available at the western end of Llyn Ogwen on the A5 and in laybys along the lake. Start the walk from the refreshment kiosk at the western end of the lake. Grid ref: SH 650 604.*

On the summit of Glyder Fawr looking to Snowdon and Crib Goch

THE TWO GIANTS OF THE GLYDER RANGE stand shoulder to shoulder, separated by a wasteland of shattered rocks and tottering spikes, giving the summit plateau a lunar-like quality. To the south the land falls away gracefully to Dyffryn Mymbyr and the Llanberis Pass, but to the north things are very different—a landscape of deep glacial cwms separated by fine rock arêtes. These peaks are second only to Snowdon in their rugged grandeur.

Approaching from the north, this route avoids a direct frontal assault on the mountain, but still samples some of its finest rock scenery.

The route: Take the well-constructed footpath which leaves the car park beside the little snack bar. Cross the footbridge and follow path until it swings right in about 400m towards Cwm Idwal. Don't follow the Idwal path, keep ahead here on a branch path, eventually rising more steeply beside the stream to reach the hanging valley of Cwm Bochlwyd with is sheltered lake. This path is known as the Miners' Track and originated as the route taken by miners from Bethesda to the mines in Cwm Dyli on Snowdon.

Ignore a branch which leads off right to ascend the rock ridge of Y Gribin, staying instead with the Miners' Track which continues above the northeastern shore of the lake to Bwlch Tryfan. Cross the stone wall which straddles the highest point of the bwlch and continue on the footpath ahead across scree to gain Glyder Fach's broad east ridge. Once you have gained the ridge turn sharp right up the final slopes—a mix of grass and jumbled rocks

There are superb views of Tryfan to the right—its narrow summit ridge seen edge-on. A short detour to Llyn Caseg-fraith is worthwhile for the superb view of Tryfan.

The summit is flat but far from unremarkable. Views southwest to Snowdon and north to Ogwen and Tryfan are superb and the summit plateau with its chaotic rocks can seem quite 'other worldly' particularly in misty conditions. The highest point—which can sometimes be difficult to decide on—lies just to the west of the famous rock table known as 'The Cantilever'.

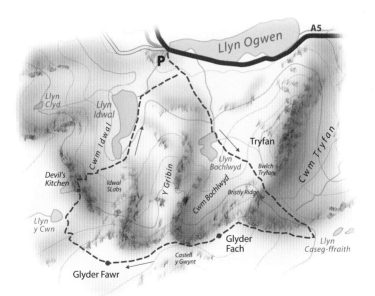

Continue west across the plateau to the equally famous Castell y Gwynt—'castle of the winds'—a group of rock spikes 'as romantic as their name'. The prospect of Snowdon with Castell y Gwynt in the foreground is one of Snowdonia's classic sights. The path skirts the rocks to the south (left) to regain the ridge where it narrows at Bwlch y Ddwy Glyder and there is a view down into Cwm Bochlwyd and across to Tryfan. From here a path rises to the right along the rim of Cwm Bochlwyd to the top of Y Gribin which could be used to shorten the route if needed, but involves scrambling (not recommended in bad conditions as the top of the ridge can be difficult to locate in poor visibility).

The path ahead continues to Glyder Fawr whose summit, like Glyder Fach, is marked by groups of spiky rock formations providing mysterious foregrounds for views of the Snowdon group.

The usual descent from Glyder Fawr is by a well-worn scree path which heads northwest and is marked regularly by cairns. In its lower reaches this is very loose and leads to the broad saddle above the Devil's Kitchen where it joins the Idwal–Nant Peris path beside Llyn y Cŵn. Turn right by the lake and follow the well constructed path steeply down beside the Devil's Kitchen into Cwm Idwal.

The Devil's Kitchen rising above Llyn Idwal

Llyn Idwal with Pen-yr Ole Wen in the background

Lower down a short detour to the left will take you to the bottom of the 'Kitchen' itself. The unpleasant slippery rocks of the gorge were first climbed by Victorian pioneer rock climbers, but such dark, damp corners are avoided by modern rock gymnasts.

Below the Devils' Kitchen the path makes its way through a jumble of massive boulders. A fork in the path partway through the boulder field marks the divide between the paths which run along the eastern and western shores of Llyn Idwal. Take your pick here, both options are similar in length and terrain. The right-hand option will take you below the impressive face known as the Idwal Slabs, returning along a formalised stone faced path to Ogwen Cottage. The left-hand option offers the best views back into the cwm across the lake.

For the latter route, bear left at the fork and follow the path down through the boulders and along the eastern shore of the lake. At the end of the lake go right along the shingle beach and cross the footbridge over the outflow. Turn left and follow the well-made footpath back to the car park.

Y Garn from Llyn Ogwen

4. Y Garn & the Devil's Kitchen from Llyn Ogwen

Outline: *An easy walk along a well constructed path to Cwm Idwal with its beautiful lake and spectacular rock scenery. This is followed by a steep climb on a good path through a huge boulder field to the sinister gorge of the Devil's Kitchen. A shattered terrace leads to easier ground and a long gradual climb takes you to the summit of Y Garn. Descent is by the steep northeast ridge.*

Distance: *7.5km/4¾ miles.*

Height gained: *690m/2,250ft.*

Summits: *Y Garn.*

Starting point: *Parking is available at the western end of Llyn Ogwen and in laybys along the lake. Start the walk from the refreshment kiosk. Grid ref: SH 650 604.*

SOMETIMES REFERRED TO AS THE 'ARMCHAIR MOUNTAIN', from the two enclosing ridges which embrace the tiny Llyn Clyd, Y Garn dominates the view west along Llyn Ogwen. Of the two ridges only the northeast ridge provides a walkable route, but it is mercilessly steep.

The route outlined below takes a more leisurely approach to the mountain via the beautiful amphitheatre of Cwm Idwal—worthy of a visit in its own right—and the famous cleft known as the 'Devil's Kitchen' (Twll Du). From there a more leisurely jaunt with fine views can be enjoyed. The steep northeast ridge—which gives stunning views into the Ogwen valley—is used as a descent.

The route: Take the well constructed footpath which leaves the car park beside the little snack bar and toilet block. For the first 400m the path heads southwest towards Tryfan, before curving right (the branch path straight ahead here is the Miner's Track which leads over the Glyderau to Pen y Pass) towards Cwm Idwal. At Llyn Idwal take the path along the left-hand shore towards the clean sweep of rock known as the Idwal slabs. The path passes directly below the slabs which are often dotted with rock climbers.

From here a stone-faced footpath veers right up the huge boulder field towards the dripping rocks of the famous Devil's Kitchen.

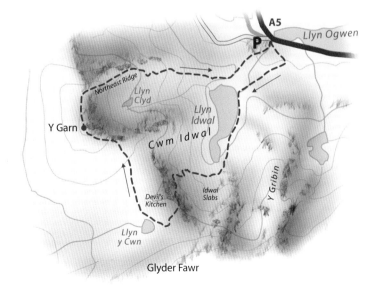

Y Garn from the shore of Llyn Idwal

Walkers starting the descent of Y Garn's northeast ridge

Immediately below the gorge, the path bends left along a shattered terrace to reach the broad rounded plateau holding Llyn y Cŵn ('lake of the dogs'). Turn right at the lake up the broad easy-angled slopes which rise to Y Garn. As you near the shoulder of the mountain, the path follows the edge of the cwm to reach the summit.

From the summit walk north along the ridge until the footpath can be seen dropping steeply down the northeast ridge (photo above). The path is quite steep and loose in places but easily followed. At about the halfway point the angle eases and you have a view to Llyn Clyd on your right. Continue down the ridge which steepens again for a while to pass close to the shore of Llyn Idwal. Return can be made by the outgoing route from the end of the lake, but a better option is to look for a path which heads left about halfway along the lake to a stile in the fence. Cross the stile and follow the path ahead over grass to cross a second stile which leads down into a small man-made gorge to emerge in the car park again.

Tryfan and Bristly Ridge from the northeast

5. The Bochlwyd Horseshoe—North Ridge of Tryfan/Bristly Ridge/Y Gribin

Outline: SCRAMBLE *Scrambling starts low down on Tryfan's North Ridge. Higher up two fine rock pitches take you onto the North Peak and finally the airy summit. After a descent of the easier and shorter South Ridge, the pinnacles of Bristly Ridge deliver you onto the rocky summit plateau of Glyder Fach. The impressive rock scenery continues with the famous Cantilever and Castell y Gwynt. Descent is by the rock ridge of Y Gribin completing the circuit of Cwm Bochlwyd.*

Distance: *6.5km/4 miles.*

Height gained: *930m/3,080ft.*

Summits: *Tryfan & Glyder Fach.*

Starting point: *Car park or laybys at the eastern end of Llyn Ogwen. Begin directly below the huge bulging buttress of rock (known as the Milestone Buttress) which has a stone wall reaching from its lowest rocks down to the road.*
Grid ref: SH 663 603.

THIS IS A SUPERB ROUTE COMBINING THE IMPRESSIVE north ridges of Tryfan and Glyder Fach. For quality of scrambling and purity of line the Bochlwyd Horseshoe can only be rivalled (and arguably not exceeded) by the Snowdon Horseshoe. The crest of Bristly Ridge provides the crux of the scrambling and there are one or two exposed sections where care is needed. Once this is behind you, you can stride out and enjoy the remaining rock scenery in the form of 'The Cantilever' and Castell y Gwynt ('Castle of the Winds') seen against an impressive back drop of the Snowdon group. Descent is by the easier but still interesting rock ridge of Y Gribin (Gribin Ridge).

The route: From the road take the footpath on the left side of the wall leading up to the Milestone Buttress. Directly below the crag, turn left on a cobbled footpath which rises to the rounded shoulder below an indistinct rock step on the right. This is the foot of the North Ridge proper.

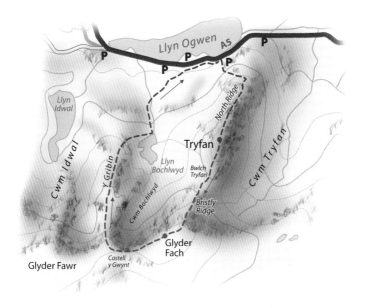

Take your pick of numerous routes which tackle the broken rocks above. The easiest line leads from the top of a scree cone directly below the broken ridge crest above. More challenging lines can be found to the right, but don't stray too far from the crest.

Unusual rock formations are very much the theme on this route and part-way up this section you will pass the first of several. Known as 'The Cannon', walkers have been climbing and photographing each other on this angled rock slab since Victorian times.

All routes converge at a broad flat shoulder with distinctive flat rock slabs. Above, the ridge continues broad and broken to a second shoulder, smaller this time but with similar rock slabs. Above lies a much steeper pyramidal buttress—the first of Tryfan's triple buttresses. There is an escape route to the left here which takes you across the shattered East Face at an easier grade (see the following route), but this still requires scrambling. Back to the North Ridge and the best scrambling is to be found taking a direct line up the pyramidal buttress with easier options to the right.

The next obstacle is the large tower of the North Peak. A direct ascent is not an option but a wide easy chimney to the right delivers you onto the summit. Move easily across the connecting ridge to the main summit of the mountain where you will encounter the next rock curiosity of the day, the twin stones known as 'Adam and Eve'. They are

The rock spike known as 'The Cannon' on the North Ridge of Tryfan

The North Ridge of Tryfan, Bristly Ridge (centre) and Y Gribin on Glyder Fach seen from Pen-yr Ole Wen across the Ogwen Valley

the sole remnants of a layer of rock which has been removed leaving these two pillars standing like the final teeth in a decaying jaw.

This is a fine mountain summit, a small rock shelf poised above the huge east face and not a blade of grass anywhere. Possibly the best summit in Snowdonia

Descend the South Ridge by a choice of routes—the main path keeps to the right of the South Peak and away from the East Face but more scrambling can be enjoyed by staying close to the crest of the ridge.

At Bwlch Tryfan you can prepare yourself for the climax of the day—one of Snowdonia's finest scrambles—Bristly Ridge. From the bwlch follow the path on the right side of the wall which rises up to the lowest rocks of the ridge above. The path soon bears diagonally-right up the scree to the foot of the rocks. There is a prominent gully above at this point. Ignore this bearing left. About 10m from the wall turn right up a short chimney with a section of wall at the top. Climb over this and turn right up a chimney above. Where the climbing becomes

Descending one of the pinnacles on Bristly Ridge with Tryfan behind

hard move onto the left wall, then move back right across the chimney to a rib which leads up to easier ground.

Continue directly up the ridge to the first small pinnacle, cross the gap and continue up to the second much larger pinnacle. The descent into the next gap can look quite intimidating. It is easier than it looks but still requires care. Climb down into the gap from the left. Pass to the right of a huge flake of rock to reach a recess behind. Climb the corner and move right onto steeper rocks to reach easier ground. The easy ridge above delivers you onto the summit plateau.

A short walk across the lunar-like landscape of the plateau will take you to the summit.

A stone's throw from the highest rocks is the famous rock table known as 'The Cantilever'. Unless you have the mountain to yourself (very rare!) there will be the usual gathering taking photographs of each other standing on the table. Even Thomas Pennant couldn't resist this over 200 years ago. His artist produced a drawing little different from the images taken home by today's walkers.

From the summit continue west along the broad ridge to another group of rocks almost as famous as 'The Cantilever'—Castell y Gwynt ('Castle of the winds'). A path avoids the rocks on the south side but taken direct they provide pleasant scrambling. Rejoin the path on the far side where it forks; bear right here (the path ahead continues to Glyder Fawr) making a short rise along the edge of Cwm Bochlwyd to the top of Y Gribin (Gribin Ridge). In poor visibility it is not always easy to locate the top of the ridge as the first few metres are quite steep and look little different to the slabs tumbling into Cwm Cneifion. In normal conditions however there should be no problem. The best scrambling is to be found near the crest with easier lines to the left.

Things become easier as you descend until the ridge widens and levels. There are superb views across Cwm Bochlwyd to Tryfan and down into Cwm Cneifion from here.

At the foot of the ridge (almost level with Llyn Bochlwyd) turn right at a crossing path (the path to the left leads down to Llyn Idwal) and follow the path to the outflow of Llyn Bochlwyd where you will meet the Miners' Track (Ogwen to Pen y Gwryd). Turn left and drop steeply beside the stream. As the angle eases a faint path bears right. This path heads across the lower slopes of Tryfan to the eastern end of Llyn Ogwen to complete the route.

The rock ridge of Y Gribin used as the descent

The East Face of Tryfan rising above Cwm Tryfan

6. *Tryfan—East Face/South Ridge /Braich Ddeugwm*

Outline: SCRAMBLE *This route takes the easier sections of the North Ridge and avoids the harder scrambling higher up by traversing the gullies of the East Face. Short sections of moderate scrambling are required on the North Ridge and in the gullies near the summit. Descent is by the easier South Ridge, followed by straightforward walking around the rim of Cwm Tryfan with superb views of Tryfan's East Face.*

Distance: *8km/5 miles.*

Height gained: *750m/2,450ft.*

Summits: *Tryfan.*

Starting point: *There is a layby on the A5 just to the east of Llyn Ogwen between the lake and the track to Gwern Gof Uchaf farm. Grid ref: SH 671 605.*

TRYFAN IS ARGUABLY THE FINEST MOUNTAIN IN SNOWDONIA. A true rock peak, it stands apart from the main bulk of the Glyder range like a giant up-turned axe blade and has delighted travellers west bound on the A5 for centuries. Few can forget their first sight of it as its great triple buttresses slide into view from behind the rounded, unremarkable shoulder of Gallt yr Ogof.

Which ever route you take to the summit you will not be able to avoid using your hands here and there. This route follows the famous North Ridge but avoids the hardest section of the scramble by turning into the gullies on the East Face where scrambling is easier and less exposed.

The route: Walk east along the A5 and turn right down the track to Gwern Gof Uchaf farm. Follow the track to the farm passing it on the left-hand side where a stile leads over the wall onto a bridleway (previously the old road through the valley). Turn right and follow the bridleway to a point level with the farm outbuildings and bear left on a footpath which heads towards Tryfan. Ignore a left turn at a fork in the path continuing ahead, then up past the prominent rock slab known as 'Little Tryfan'. Immediately after the slab the path bears right up over small rock ribs to a stile over the fence giving access to the Cwm

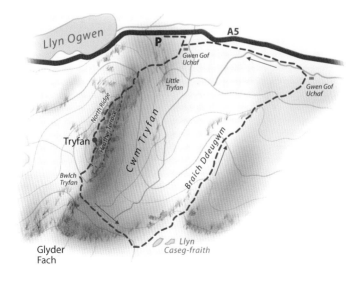

The East Face of Tryfan from Llyn Caseg-fraith

Tryfan path. Don't cross this stile, instead, take the path to the right and walk up parallel to the fence. Higher up the path rises by stone steps through a short gully.

At the top of the gully don't take the path immediately left which leads onto Heather Terrace, instead, continue ahead a little further onto the shoulder of the mountain. You are now at the foot of the famous North Ridge which can be tackled by a number of lines—the easiest follows a ribbon of scree and boulders directly below the broken ridge crest above. All routes converge at a broad shoulder with distinctive flat rock slabs.

Above the shoulder, the ridge continues broken and indistinct to a second level area, smaller this time but with similar flat rock slabs. Above lies a much steeper pyramidal buttress—the first of Tryfan's triple buttresses. The North Ridge route tackles this buttress direct, but the East Face route (which is a little easier and less exposed) turns this obstacle on the left to begin a traverse of the gullies.

The path rises leftwards well below the crest of the North Ridge and requires some scrambling. The path now traverses the upper section of a gully, then scrambles up to reach a notch immediately below the

North Peak. Continue across the gully beyond the notch where a similar scramble brings you to the summit beside the famous twin rocks of Adam and Eve.

The summit is a superb spot with grand views and Adam and Eve perched impressively on the very edge of the huge east face of the mountain.

Descend the South Ridge passing the South Peak over to the left and cross the small saddle to Far South Peak. The next larger saddle is Bwlch Tryfan—the watershed between Cwm Tryfan and Cwm Bochlwyd. Ahead rise the rocks of Bristly Ridge and the northern cliffs of Glyder Fach. The Miners' Track, a path linking Ogwen with Pen y Gwryd, crosses the ridge here at its lowest point and continues across the screes to the left to reach the rounded shoulder of Glyder Fach. Follow this path left to the shoulder and then bear left to the scattering of small lakes (Llyn Caseg-fraith). Beyond the lakes locate the top of Braich y Ddeugwm, the long finger-like ridge forming the eastern bounds of Cwm Tryfan.

There is a footpath here but it is faint and could be very difficult to find in poor visibility. In good visibility no path is needed—once on the ridge the walking is a delight with springy turf underfoot and stunning views across Cwm Tryfan to the East Face of Tryfan and Bristly Ridge.

The ridge ends above Gwern Gof Isaf farm. Pass the farm and walk down the access track towards the road. Just before the bridge turn left along the right of way which follows the line of the old road through the valley back to Gwern Gof Uchaf farm.

(A shorter route from the summit of Tryfan can be made by returning via Heather Terrace—the prominent terrace which crosses the east face of the mountain. For this option follow the South Ridge to the saddle between the South Peak and Far South Peak. Cross the stile over the wall here and descend the scree which falls into Cwm Tryfan. About halfway down the scree look for a cairned path on the left (easily missed). This marks the end of Heather Terrace, the feature which is so obvious from the valley but not so obvious when you are on the mountain trying to locate it. Follow the path along the terrace which soon becomes better established. The terrace eventually leads to the short gully used on the ascent at the foot of the North Ridge. Bear right down the gully and return via Little Tryfan to Gwern Gof Uchaf farm.)

Snowdon (Yr Wyddfa) and Crib Goch

7. *Snowdon by Cwm Dyli—Pyg Track/Miners' Track*

Outline: *A gradual climb along the rocky but well constructed Pyg Track leads to Bwlch Moch. From here you enter the Snowdon Horseshoe with its grand scenery. Old mine workings add extra interest, before the final climb up the famous 'Zig-zags' to join the Snowdon Mountain Railway and the Llanberis Path, which is followed to the summit. Descent is by a return to the 'Zig-zags' and a steep rocky Miners' Track to Glaslyn and Llyn Llydaw. A good, almost level path, returns to Pen-y-Pass.*

Distance: *12km/7½ miles.*

Height gained: *914m/3,000ft.*

Summits: *Snowdon (Yr Wyddfa).*

Start: *There is a moderate sized car park at Pen-y-Pass where the route starts (often full early during the summer). A fee is payable. Grid ref: SH 647 557. Alternatively, use the park and ride at Nant Peris to reach Pen-y-Pass. Grid ref: SH 606 584.*

FEW WOULD BEGRUDGE CWM DYLI'S CLAIM to being Snowdon's most impressive and dramatic valley. But it is also the mountain's best known and has been painted and photographed since the first visitors began to come to Snowdonia almost two centuries ago. The cwm is enclosed by the rocky arms of the famous 'Snowdon Horseshoe' producing one of the most appealing mountain views in Britain. The grand scenery is enhanced by two mountain lakes, the upper lake—Glaslyn—is cradled in an impressive rock basin with the summit cone rising almost 500 metres (about 1,600 feet) above its green waters.

Sadly Cwm Dyli has also been despoiled since the mid-nineteenth century by mining activities, but it remains one of the finest approaches to the mountain.

The route: From the Pen-y-Pass car park the obvious exit from the lower car park is the Miners' Track, the Pyg Track exits from the higher car park just behind the cafe ('Gorphwysfa Restaurant') through a gap in the stone wall and under power lines. The Pyg Track is well constructed and easily followed to Bwlch Moch, the point at which it enters the Snowdon Horseshoe.

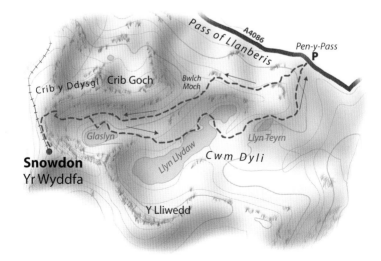

From here there are views down to Llyn Llydaw and it's causeway, and beyond to the 300m/1,000ft face of Y Lliwedd. Ahead is Snowdon looking deceptively close.

Ignore the path to the right here, this is the steep path leading up to Crib Goch, the Pyg Track continues over the stiles ahead to contour along the mountain's southern slopes. Following the Pyg Track, you eventually reach a superb viewpoint where Glaslyn and the dramatic summit cone of Snowdon can be seen to perfection rising above the lake.

Continue on the contouring path to an even closer viewpoint directly above Glaslyn. From here the path curves around the cwm passing the junction with the Miners' Track (marked by an upright stone—take note of this for the descent) coming up from the left and the remains of the copper mines. Higher up you reach the foot of the famous 'Zig-zags' which negotiate the final steep slopes to Bwlch Glas. The bwlch is marked by a two-metre upright stone pillar and it is here you meet with the Llanberis Path and the Snowdon Mountain Railway. Turn left for the final ten-minute walk to the summit.

Yr Wyddfa, the summit of Snowdon, from the Pyg Track

Looking down into Cwm Dyli from the top of the 'Zig-zags'

To descend, return to the standing stone on Bwlch Glas and descend the 'Zig-zags'. As the angle eases the path swings leftwards taking a more gradual traversing line with mining remains below. Look for the junction with the Miners' Track noted on the ascent and marked by an upright stone pillar. This path descends directly down a wide scree gully to the shore of Glaslyn. (Avoid a path which breaks away slightly earlier and takes a more diagonal line passing close to mines before reaching the lake.)

Descend to Glaslyn and follow the path along the shore to the outflow. The path continues beside the stream to the shores of Llyn Llydaw, then along the northern shore of the lake and across the stone causeway originally built by miners working in the Glaslyn Mines during the nineteenth century. Beyond the causeway the path is virtually level and wide—almost a road—and contours the slopes back to Pen-y-Pass.

Looking into Cwm Dyli from Crib y Ddysgl

8. *The Snowdon Horseshoe—*

Outline: **SCRAMBLE** *This magnificent route provides moderate, exposed scrambling for much of its length with one or two sections where a fall could be serious. The most demanding section will be found on the Crib Goch Pinnacles with the return leg over Y Lliwedd offering grand views from the top of the largest precipice in Wales. This section involves rough, rocky walking rather than the type of scrambling encountered on Crib Goch.*

Distance: *11.5km/7¼ miles.*

Height gained: *1,180m/3,850ft.*

Summits: *Crib Goch, Crib y Ddysgl, Snowdon & Y Lliwedd.*

Start: *There is a moderate sized car park at Pen-y-Pass where the route starts (often full early during the summer). A fee is payable. Grid ref: SH 647 557. Alternatively, use the park and ride located at Nant Peris to reach Pen-y-Pass. Grid ref: SH 606 584.*

THE SNOWDON HORSESHOE OFFERS A MAGNIFICENT MOUNTAIN DAY—possibly the best scramble south of the Scottish Highlands. It follows the skyline of Cwm Dyli formed by the two great eastern ridges of Y Lliwedd and the infamous Crib Goch.

The cautionary note in the outline paragraph should be noted by anyone unsure of their ability in situations of exposed scrambling. Crib Goch is a rock peak and you can not reach its summit without scrambling, although the standard is not high and should be within the ability of most individuals. Under ice and snow this route becomes a low-end winter climb and should be treated as such.

The route: Take the Pyg Track, a well constructed path—with views down the Llanberis Pass—to Bwlch Moch, the point at which you enter the Snowdon Horseshoe. The obvious exit from the lower car park is the Miners' Track, the Pyg Track exits from the higher car park just behind the café ('Gorphwysfa Restaurant') through a gap in the stone wall and beneath power lines.

From Bwlch Moch there are superb views down to Llyn Llydaw and it's causeway, and beyond to the 300m face of Y Lliwedd. Ahead is Snowdon looking deceptively close. Here the path forks. The Pyg

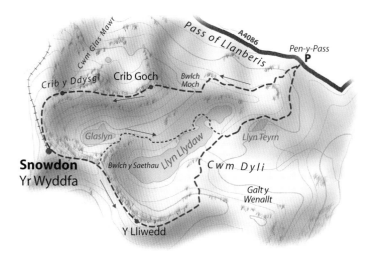

Track continues over stiles ahead to contour the southern slopes of Crib Goch, whilst the Crib Goch path bears right taking a steeper line up over the shoulder. The path has recently been pitched making it almost impossible to miss.

Higher up your way is barred by a large, broken rock step guarding the foot of the East Ridge. The left-hand side of this step is both steep and hard, while the right-hand side eventually merges into the shattered east face of the mountain. The most frequented line is almost direct, a little right of centre and involves moderate rock scrambling up a series of grooves and corners. Once above the rock step the easier rocks of the upper East Ridge lead spectacularly to the summit.

This is one of the most dramatic places in Snowdonia and if you can relax it is a good place to rest and enjoy the fantastic scenery that surrounds you. The knife edge of the North Ridge sweeps down into the Llanberis Pass to the right, but it is likely to be the narrow ridge ahead which will grab your attention. The views are magnificent, particularly to Snowdon which stands impressively beyond the pinnacles.

The ridge is very narrow, almost level and exposed for about 300m. It is usual on this section to drop down a metre or so on the left side of the ridge and use the crest for hand holds which will also give you a little protection from the exposure on the north side.

Traversing the narrow crest of Crib Goch

Looking along Crib Goch towards the 'Pinnacles ' and Snowdon

The ridge eventually leads to the first of the famous 'Pinnacles'. These can be tackled direct or more usually turned on the left by an obvious traversing path, but be careful not to descend too far. From the gap before the final (third) pinnacle there is a short exposed scramble on the north side overlooking a gully and requiring care, but once over this section the descent to Bwlch Coch is straightforward. The major difficulties are now behind you.

The ridge is now much wider, far less exposed and rises to one last rock step on the approach to Crib y Ddysgl. Beyond the rock step a short, narrow section just before the summit is normally turned on the right.

From Crib y Ddysgl follow the edge of Cwm Dyli to Bwlch Glas (marked by a 2-metre upright stone) where you join the Llanberis Path and the routes coming up the 'Zig-zags' from Glaslyn. A short easy walk of about ten minutes will take you to the summit.

If you enjoy crowds, the new summit visitor centre is the place to lunch, otherwise you will want to be on your way. Descend the upper section of the South Ridge for about 150m to reach the upright stone

Approaching the summit of Crib y Ddysgl

(similar to the one on Bwlch Glas) which marks the point where the Watkin Path leaves the ridge. Turn left and follow the Watkin Path which takes a diagonal line across the south face of the mountain to Bwlch y Saethau where the path almost levels.

(Here you can cut the route short if needed by scrambling down Y Gribin—a moderate rock ridge which drops to Glaslyn. The standard is a little easier than Crib Goch, technically harder than continuing over Y Lliwedd, but easier on tired knees. The main problem in descent, as with all such routes, is locating the top of the ridge. In good visibility you will know that you are in the correct location as the entire ridge is visible below. In poor visibility the route is best avoided without prior knowledge.

For Y Gribin bear left at Bwlch y Saethau to the edge of the cwm above Glaslyn. There is a small pool amongst the grass and rocks here—not the only one unfortunately—with a narrow but visible path leading diagonally down to the start of the ridge. This point is marked by a small cairn.

As already mentioned in clear conditions you will see the ridge below you curving down to the outflow of Glaslyn. The best line keeps to the crest and avoids both the extreme right-hand side where the cliffs fall alarmingly to Llyn Llydaw and the left where the scrambling is poor. Turn right along the Miners' Track and follow it down to cross Llyn Llydaw by the causeway and back to Pen-y-Pass.)

To continue over Y Lliwedd from Bwlch y Saethau, follow the Watkin Path down to Bwlch Ciliau (the lowest point on the ridge between Snowdon and Y Lliwedd) where it turns right at a junction down into Cwm Llan. Keep ahead here on the path which follows the edge of the cliffs to Y Lliwedd which can be seen rising dramatically ahead.

The summit is a dramatic place to be—the huge north face of the mountain being the highest precipice in Wales. The views are magnificent, particularly back to Snowdon and across the void of Cwm Dyli to Crib Goch with Llyn Llydaw below.

To continue, cross the mountain's twin summits on a good path which heads down the east ridge and over a lower sub top aptly named Lliwedd Bach (*'little Lliwedd'*). The path levels at a shoulder just before some small pools, then bears left down into Cwm Dyli to the outflow of Llyn Llydaw where you join the Miners' Track. Turn right and follow the Miners' Track back to Pen-y-Pass.

The twin summits of Y Lliwedd with Snowdon (Yr Wyddfa) behind

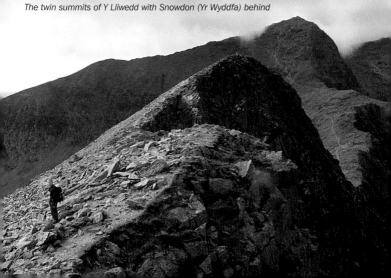

Snowdon (Yr Wyddfa) rising above Cwm Llan

9. Cwm Llan Horseshoe— Y Lliwedd/South Ridge/Yr Aran

Outline: *A beautiful approach through woods to a remote hanging valley is followed by a spectacular ridge walk. The final rise to Snowdon is over steep scree but is more than compensated for by the easy jaunt down the South Ridge with its spectacular views and the option to include the shapely summit of Yr Aran.*

Distance: *16km/10 miles.*

Height gained: *1,150m/3760ft.*

Summits: *Y Lliwedd, Snowdon (Yr Wyddfa) & Yr Aran.*

Starting point: *Pont Bethania car park near Nantgwynant on the A498 road to Beddgelert. Grid ref: SH 628 506.*

THE MAIN ATTRACTION OF THIS ROUTE is the beautiful approach through woods and beside the cascading Afon Cwm Llan to the remote hanging valley of Cwm Merch and the superb viewpoint of Gallt y Wenallt. The traverse of Y Lliwedd is spectacular, passing along the edge of the highest precipice in Wales.

The descent from Snowdon by the South Ridge has the advantage of being slightly off the normal 'trade routes' and thus less crowded. It is also a fine ridge, particularly in the upper half where it narrows to form the famous 'Saddle' at Bwlch Main. If you still have the energy, Yr Aran makes a fine finish for the day.

The route: Turn left out of the car park, cross the bridge and in about 100m or so turn right into a narrow lane. Don't follow the lane which leads to the farms of Hafod-y-llan, instead, go up stone steps immediately ahead, signed for the 'Watkin Path'. This new section of path weaves through mature woods above the lane to eventually join the old route—now a rough track—with a view out over the valley. Go left through the gate (signed 'Watkin') and follow the rising track, soon with the cascading Afon Cwm Llan down to your right. The path soon swings left with a view ahead to waterfalls and the remains of an old incline rising steeply up the hillside. Follow path, eventually crossing the incline and a little further on, immediately before a gate, turn right and walk beside the wall down to an old stone slab bridge.

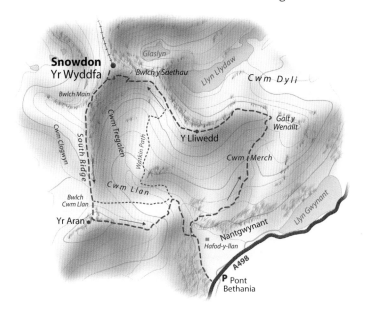

On the summit of Gallt y Wenallt, with Snowdon and Crib Goch behind

Cross the bridge and go ahead up the bank ignoring a stile and gate to the left. A little higher up a second stile by a gate leads onto an old mining road—now a pleasant green track—which leads through oak woods and scattered pines. This section is a delight. All too soon the trees thin out and after a stile by a gate in the wall, disappear altogether. The path continues to climb, eventually zig-zaging up to a gateway in a wall. Go through the gateway and follow the path as it turns sharp left, then sharp right.

The path climbs gently for a while then levels to contour beside an old wall, eventually bringing you to the abandoned mines in the broad shallow hanging valley of Cwm Merch. Just before the ruins, take a narrow footpath which bears left off the main path (if you reach the mine buildings you have gone too far). This very soon becomes vague so scramble up left for a few metres over a rocky stream to a level area beside a ruin. Bear right above the ruin and pick up a path which crosses the rust-coloured spoil from the workings above. Continue ahead now on a vague grassy path to the saddle on the skyline.

Looking down from the summit of Y Lliwedd to Llyn Llydaw

The minor top of Gallt y Wenallt lies to the right—worth the short detour for the stunning view—otherwise turn left on the path which hugs the edge of the cliffs rising above Cwm Dyli. The steepening path is easily followed now to Y Lliwedd's twin summits, perched impressively above a 300m/1,000ft face—the largest cliff face in Wales.

From here the descent along the ridge is obvious to Bwlch Cilau where the Watkin Path joins from the left *(a possible return if time is short)*. Follow the path ahead to Bwlch y Saethau ('pass of the arrows')—a name associating the place with King Arthur—before the final steep rise to Snowdon.

At the time of writing the path is quite eroded and negotiates the steep scree-covered southern face of the mountain to join the South Ridge at an upright stone just below the summit which lies up to the right.

From the summit return along the South Ridge passing the upright stone. A little further on it narrows considerably at the famous Bwlch Main, sometimes known as 'The Saddle'. The ridge is interesting here rather than spectacular and there are fine airy views into both Cwm Clogwyn on the right and Cwm Tregalen to the left with a moderate amount of exposure. After Bwlch Main there is a short rise to a subsidiary top then an enjoyable easy descent to Bwlch Cwm Llan, the pass which separates the South Ridge from Yr Aran, Snowdon's shapely southern satellite.

On the South Ridge near Bwlch Main

On the lower section of the South Ridge with Yr Aran in the background

(From here the shortest route is to turn left and follow the path down to and then along the course of an old tramway until you are above the ruins of Plas Cwm Llan were a path heads steeply down to join the Watkin Path at its exit from Cwm Llan. Turn right and follow the Watkin Path back to Pont Bethania.)

Alternatively, if you have any energy left you can include Yr Aran. For this option take the path ahead up beside the wall. This swings left below the final rocks where you join the east ridge. Go right for the summit.

Retrace your steps back down to the wall and follow it east along the ridge. Where the wall turns south almost at the ridge end (GR. 614 515) turn left and descend steeply beside mines on the right. Head down northeast now over rough ground to reach the old tramway near GR. 619 519. Depending on where you joined the tramway (ideally just after it has crossed the stream and where it is supported on one side by stonework) you may have to turn left, right or go straight across on a path which descends to join the Watkin Path. Turn right and follow the Watkin Path back to Pont Bethania.

Trum y Ddysgl from the shoulder of Craig Cwm Silyn

10. *The Nantlle Ridge*

Outline: *After a short, steep climb to gain the first peak, the ridge is pure delight. There are one or two sections with easy scrambling on Mynydd Drws-y-coed, but the most of the ridge is rounded and grassy with wide views to Lleyn, the sea and back to Snowdon.*

Distance: *14km/8¾ miles.*

Height gained: *1,200m/3,900ft.*

Summits: *Y Garn, Mynydd Drws-y-coed, Trum y Ddysgl, Mynydd Tal-y-mignedd & Craig Cwm Silyn.*

Starting point: *The village of Rhyd-Ddu on the A4085 Caernarfon to Beddgelert road. There are car parks for Snowdon immediately south of the village. Grid ref: SH 571 526.*

THE WALL OF HILLS WHICH RISE TO THE SOUTH of Nantlle are linked conveniently by a graceful sweeping ridge which provides one of Snowdonia's finest mountain walks. Only two points on the ridge exceed 700 metres, but what these hills lack in height they certainly make up for in their rugged and often dramatic outlines.

As a mountain ridge walk, the Nantlle Ridge can probably only be bettered by the Snowdon Horseshoe. But there is a problem. Although all the summits are connected with minimum loss of height, it is hard to make a satisfying circular walk. The options are: to walk it as a linear route and arrange transport at both ends; walk it in both directions; retrace your steps to the central summit of Trum y Ddysgl, descending the south ridge to Bwlch-y-Ddwy-elor and then return through Beddgelert Forest; descend into the head of Cwm Pennant from Bwlch Dros-bern and then head for Bwlch-y-Ddwy-elor avoiding the ascents back along the ridge, but much of the terrain is pathless.

The route: Opposite the car park entrance a kissing gate leads onto a footpath paved with flat stones which crosses a damp, flat field with the dramatic profile of Y Garn, the northeastern terminus of the Nantlle Ridge, directly ahead. At a stream bear left to a footbridge with a stone cottage on the right. Cross the driveway and shortly join it again a little further on continuing to the road (B4418).

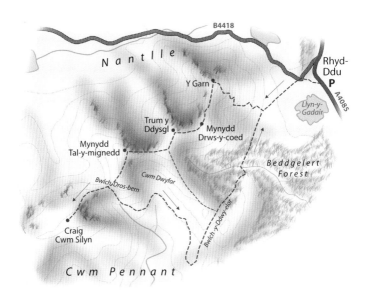

The approach to Mynydd Tal-y-mignedd. Craig Cwm Silyn lies in the distance

Don't go onto the road, instead, take the signed footpath on the left which initially passes along field edges with the dramatic outlines of Y Garn and Mynydd Drws-y-coed rising ahead. After a stream the path curves right and begins the steep climb to the first summit—Y Garn. After a large rock with white arrows painted on it the path divides. Ignore the path ahead which continues through the forest to Bwlch-y-Ddwy-elor and Cwm Pennant (used as one of the return options), instead, bear right rising steeply and directly up the eastern slopes of Y Garn.

After a long stiff pull the angle begins to ease and just before the highest point a well-built stone wall is cross by a ladder stile. The summit cairn lies a few metres to the northwest perched on the very edge of the cliffs falling into Dyffryn Nantlle (take care in poor visibility).

The view from here and throughout the walk is extensive taking in the western slopes of Snowdon and the dramatic southern face of Mynydd Mawr which dominates the opposite side of Dyffryn Nantlle. However, your eye is most likely to be drawn by the imposing profile rising along the ridge to the south. Mynydd Drws-y-coed is often seen as a hazy silhouette against the midday sun and can look quite intimidating, but don't despair, the ridge presents little more than a brief, enjoyable (and avoidable) scramble.

The path heads south, soon beside the wall crossed near the summit. Stay by the wall as the ridge narrows and soon you begin to use your hands here and there. The climax of the scrambling comes in the short final rise to Mynydd Drws-y-coed. There is exposure here but only on the right-hand side of the ridge. If big drops are not your thing keep to the left where alternative lines avoid both exposure and scrambling.

All too soon (or thankfully, depending on your viewpoint) the scrambling is over and the ridge continues as a fine narrow grass edge. After a short descent to the saddle the ridge rises impressively to Trum y Ddysgl. The best option is along the ridge crest but a slightly easier line forks left just above the saddle to emerge at the mountain's western top. (From this point note the south ridge—a broad grassy arm which descends steeply to Bwlch-y-Ddwy-elor and can be used as a return to Rhyd-Ddu).

If you stayed with the ridge crest you will arrive at the eastern top where you get a fine view back along the ridge with Snowdon in the distance. From Trum y Ddysgl the ridge continues due west narrowing at one point almost enough to require a few scrambling moves (almost). The next top, Mynydd Tal-y-mignedd is distinctive for its stone obelisk, built to celebrate Queen Victoria's Diamond Jubilee. From here the ridge continues as a broad grass plateau before a descent down broken slopes to Bwlch Dros-bern.

The next summit, Craig Cwm Silyn, marks the highest point of the traverse. A direct ascent provides an easy scramble similar in standard to that encountered on Mynydd Drws-y-coed. Easier lines avoiding the scramble lie to the right.

Although the highest point on the ridge, this is probably the least impressive summit—a broad rocky plateau reminiscent of the Glyderau. For impressive scenery you should head north to the edge of the plateau for a view of Craig Cwm Silyn, a popular rock climbing crag of huge proportions.

Mynydd Tal-y-mignedd from the descent into Cwm Pennant

There are now three main options.

1. If you are walking the ridge as a linear route continue to the final summit of Garnedd Goch—an easy 2km/1 mile stroll across the plateau, the final stages beside a wall which leads directly to the summit (a useful landmark in poor visibility). From here head west to Cors y Llyn to finish near the village of Nebo.

2. If you intend to walk the ridge as a double traverse (both ways) the extra 4km/2mile out-and-back walk to Garnedd Goch will seem a waste of valuable energy and time. The true character of the ridge ends here. Retrace your steps back to Y Garn and descend to Rhyd-Ddu.

3. There are two options for a circular walk both using Bwlch-y-Ddwy-elor to return to Rhyd-Ddu but neither are particularly satisfying. The toughest but simplest is to return along the ridge to the western shoulder of Trum y Ddysgl and descend the broad grassy south ridge to the bwlch.

Alternatively, for less height gain, retrace your steps to Bwlch Dros-bern, the last bwlch (directly below the east ridge of Craig Cwm Silyn). From here drop into the cwm to the south (right). Keep to the left-hand side of the stream and where this steepens into a small 'V'-shaped gorge curve leftwards into the adjacent cwm—Cwm Dwyfor.

There are mining remains in the bottom of the cwm here. Look for the bed of an old rail line where it passes through a crossing wall (GR. 541 503) and follow it as it contours out of the cwm and across the hillside. This can be overgrown and quite wet in places. In about 600m at GR. 545 498, and immediately after crossing a stream, turn left and head up through bracken on an indistinct path. At mines turn left up an old incline, then bear right with the path to continue the climb to Bwlch-y-Ddwy-elor.

From the bwlch a gate leads into the woods and a good path goes ahead through the trees. Eventually you reach a T junction. Turn right then left. At the next T junction turn left over a concrete bridge and turn right immediately onto a footpath beside the stream. At a crossing forest road take the path ahead, soon leaving the woods to traverse the lower slopes of Mynydd Drws-y-coed. At the path junction with the painted arrows on the rock passed earlier keep ahead and retrace the outward journey.

Looking east along the ridge From Craig Cwm Silyn to Trum y Ddysgl with Snowdon in the distance

Moel Siabod from Afon Llugwy

11. *Moel Siabod from Capel Curig—*
Daear Ddu Ridge

Outline: SCRAMBLE (easy) *A steady ascent on goods paths and farm tracks past old quarry workings to an impressive hanging valley. This is followed by a fine steep ridge with occasional scrambling in a superb setting. Easier options are always available and all scrambling is avoidable. Descent is either by the long rounded northeast ridge on good paths to join the outward route, or the gentle northern slopes above Capel Curig.*

Distance: *9km/5½ miles.*

Height gained: *760m/2,500ft.*

Summits: *Moel Siabod.*

Starting point: *A small car park beside Bryn Glo café on the A5 in Capel Curig. Grid ref: SH 735 572.*

UNLIKE THE MAJORITY OF SNOWDONIA'S HIGH MOUNTAINS, Moel Siabod presents a gentle characterless face to the north saving its charms for the southeastern approach. As a result the mountain is scarcely noticed from Capel Curig as all eyes are drawn by the Snowdon Horseshoe. By contrast, the shapely southeastern slopes are almost unrecognisable as the same mountain as they rise above Glyn Lledr—a fine pointed summit, a deeply-cut cwm with imposing headwall and a narrow rock ridge leading directly to the summit.

This route uses the fine Daear Ddu Ridge to provide an interesting route to the summit and the mountain's more gentle northerly slopes for an easy descent.

The route: Turn right out of the car park and walk along the A5 towards Capel Curig. Turn left into a minor lane crossing Afon Llugwy by the old stone bridge (Pont Cyfyng). Walk along the lane to houses (about 100m), then bear right over a cattle grid and up a steep farm road signed to 'Moel Siabod'. Follow the road steeply and where this turns sharp right to the farm higher up, take the signed footpath straight

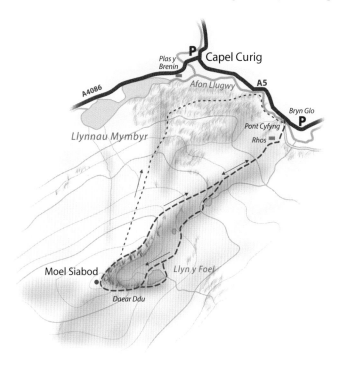

Moel Siabod and Glyn Lledr showing the Daear Ddu Ridge

ahead. The footpath joins the track which leads from the farm onto the high pastures. Turn left here and follow this track over the moors with the pyramidal peak of Moel Siabod rising ahead.

Higher up the footpath runs beside a small lake, then rises more steeply passing spoil heaps and ruined miners' cottages. Pass a small but deep water-filled quarry and rise to a broad saddle overlooking the secluded Llyn y Foel below the impressive headwall of the cwm. The Daear Ddu Ridge can now be seen for the first time rising impressively from the far side of the lake.

The most direct route to the base of the ridge is directly ahead keeping to the right of the lake, but for better views of the cwm and the ridge bear left around the lake passing over the outflow. For the best scrambling keep to the right-hand side of the ridge almost overlooking the cwm. Any difficulties can be turned on the left and easier ground can always reached by moving left. It is also possible to avoid the scrambling altogether by following the footpath well over to the left. The ridge leads directly to the summit.

Views from the summit are wide in clear conditions particularly the dramatic view west into the Snowdon Horseshoe. To the north stand the rounded backs of the Glyderau and Carneddau, with Tryfan peeping over the ridge. To the south you have the dramatic fall to Llyn y Foel, with the hills of southern Snowdonia stretching out beyond Glyn Lledr.

From the summit, head northeast along the broad rocky ridge and descend the clear path at the eastern end. Keep on down the ridge which becomes grassier as you descend to join the outward route.

(Alternatively, you can take the Capel Curig path which leaves the summit ridge about halfway along [immediately before the rocky section] and heads north [left] to pass through the woods of Coed Bryn-engan. In the lower section of the woods at a prominent T junction turn right and follow the forest road to eventually walk beside Afon Llugwy. A good path then stays beside the river passing through two grazing fields to reach the lane by the bridge [Pont Cyfyng].)

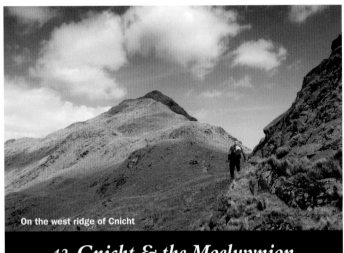

On the west ridge of Cnicht

12. Cnicht & the Moelwynion from Croesor

Outline: *A steady ascent on good paths up a long grass ridge and a short easy scramble lead to the summit of Cnicht. This is followed by a leisurely walk to Llyn yr Adar and down to Bwlch y Rhosydd. You then have the option of a long easy walk down Cwm Croesor to complete the round, or a climb through quarry spoil to reach Moelwyn Mawr and Moelwyn Bach.*

Distance: *14.5km/9 miles (longest option).*

Height gained: *1,080m/3,560ft.*

Summits: *Cnicht, Moelwyn Mawr, Craigysgafn & Moelwyn Bach.*

Starting point: *National Park car park (free at the time of writing) in the village of Croesor. Grid ref: SH 631 447.*

FEW TRAVELLERS ON THE A498 BETWEEN TREMADOG AND BEDDGELERT can fail to be impressed by the striking pyramidal peak glimpsed through occasional gaps in the trees. Like a child's drawing it rises to a perfect point and is fittingly referred to as the 'Welsh Matterhorn'.

Cnicht's less striking neighbours are often overlooked in favour of the baby of the group, but they can easily be combined to form an excellent mountain day.

The route: Turn right out of the car park and follow the rising lane out of the village. Beyond a gate the lane continues as a stoney track which twists between tiny walled fields and through open woods. Where the track levels bear right onto a good footpath which heads directly towards Cnicht's pointed summit. Higher up near a small ruin, bear right as directed by a waymarker post to cross a stile over the wall on the skyline. The path now stays more or less on the crest of the ridge to the flat grassy shoulder directly below the summit.

From here there is a short easy scramble up a slanting rake immediately to the right of the rocky ridge crest, or easier ground further right avoids all scrambling. A short section of ridge above this leads to the summit with its stunning views.

Continue east along the summit ridge over a second top then on towards the broad grass plateau which lies at the heart of the Moelwynion. In fine weather this is a beautiful spot, scattered with sparkling lakes reflecting a wide sky, with almost every peak in Snowdonia visible.

The path is well used and visible on the ground. As you approach Llyn yr Adar—which should be to your left and provides a superb foreground for the view into Snowdon's southern cwms—the path forks at a cairn. Bear right here following the path between rocky outcrops separated by grassy hollows—complicated terrain in poor visibility. The path is visible on the ground but disappears here and there. Soon you will see Llyn Cwm-y-Foel contained by its dam way down to your right and ahead the smaller islanded Llynnau Diffwys. Head for this lake passing it on the left and a smaller lake just beyond. Immediately after this turn left down to the old quarry road on Bwlch y Rhosydd, the watershed separating Cwmorthin and Cwm Croesor.

The famous view of Cnicht from the old marshlands of Traeth Mawr

Approaching the shoulder on Cnicht's west ridge

(The easiest return from Bwlch y Rhosydd is to turn right along the quarry road and where this swings right on the lip of Cwm Croesor, bear left down to join the visible path which contours the lower slopes of Moelwyn Mawr back to Croesor.)

To extend the walk to Moelwyn Mawr, turn left along the track to the ruined mine buildings associated with the nearby Rhosydd Quarry workings. Turn right up the disused incline immediately to the left of a large spoil heap. Higher up continue to the right of spoil heaps to join the broad ridge separating Moel-yr-hydd from Moelwyn Mawr with quarries to the right. Turn right and follow the ridge up to the summit.

If you are still fighting fit you can continue south over Craigysgafn and take in Moelwyn Bach (see page 70).

(Alternatively, head northwest along the ridge crest to descend the mountain's west ridge. In the lower section the angle eases and the ridge broadens. Look for a farm track visible down to the left and head for this. The track leads down to the lane where a right turn will take you back to Croesor.)

To include Craigysgafn and Moelwyn Bach, walk due east from the summit for 100m or so before turning south down towards the rocky subsidiary summit of Craigysgafn with Llyn Stwlan below.

Cross the rocky crest of Craigysgafn and drop to Bwlch Stwlan directly below the imposing block which guards any direct approach to Moelwyn Bach. Walk left along the constructed track which crosses the bwlch, before turning right on a path which then heads diagonally-left up the scree. This path leads quickly to the summit—lower, more grassy and lacking the fine ridge of its larger twin, but sharing its stunning views. The descent down the mountain's broad grassy west ridge is a delight. Springy turf sooths aching joints and a stunning view out to sea delights the eye.

At the bottom of the ridge head for the right-hand corner of a conifer wood. Go through the gate and follow the path through the trees to the lane and turn right to return to Croesor.

On the summit ridge of Moelwyn Mawr

Looking north across Llyn Hywel to Rhinog Fach and Rhinog Fawr

13. *Rhinog Fach & Y Llethr from Cwm Nantcol*

Outline: *Easy walking to Bwlch Drws Ardudwy—an ancient route through the hills—is followed by a rise to the picturesque Llyn Cwmhosan. Above this the going gets tougher as the final rougher slopes are negotiated. This is followed by the fine rocky ridge linking Rhinog Fach to Y Llethr—the highest point in the Rhinog—with its superb views back across Llyn Hywel to Rhinog Fach. An easy descent of Y Llethr's broad west ridge makes a perfect finish for tired legs.*

Distance: *11.75km/7½ miles.*

Height gained: *780m/2,550ft.*

Summits: *Rhinog Fach & Y Llethr.*

Starting point: *There is a small parking area at the head of Cwm Nantcol near the farm Maes-y-garnedd. A small fee is charged by the farm. Grid ref: SH 641 269.*

THE ENTRANCE TO CWM NANTCOL is a superb introduction to the wilds of the Rhinog. A gated lane leads either from the village of Llanbedr, or, even better, from Dyffryn Ardudwy where you are treated to a superb panorama of Rhinog Fawr, Rhinog Fach and the high point of the range, Y Llethr, as you turn into the cwm. The absence of a lake here has denied the cwm the popularity of its neighbour, but if anything Cwm Nantcol is more impressive.

The route: At the end of the tarmac lane where it swings right into the farm go ahead (ignoring the track on the left) beneath overhead cables to cross the stream by stepping stones. A good path now heads up towards the bwlch ahead, close by the wall on the right.

The path, like its more famous neighbour (Roman Steps), is paved here and there by stone slabs easing your passage over the wetter

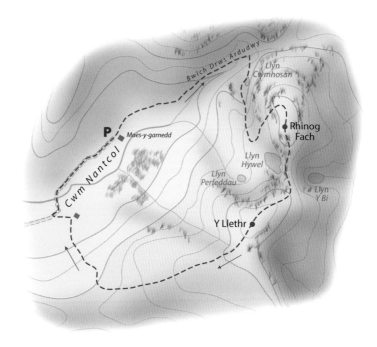

Rhinog Fawr from Llyn Cwmhosan

areas and continues ahead leaving the wall at one point near a marshy area. As you get higher the hillsides on either side close in and higher still you pass a prominent rock streaked by white quartz. You will notice a stile over the wall down to the right here which marks the start of the direct path to Llyn Hywel. Ignore this continuing a little further to where the valley levels and widens out shortly before the summit of the pass. Cross a marshy area by stepping stones and bear right to a second stile over the wall. Cross the stile and take the steep narrow path up through the heather to Llyn Cwmhosan.

This lake is one of the gems of the Rhinog. The view from the far shore looking back towards Rhinog Fawr is superb and shows the twisted layering of the mountain's ancient rocks to perfection.

The path passes to the right of the lake, then swings right over a small heathery rise to join another path at a T junction. Turn left and follow this path up below the western slopes of the mountain. As the gradient eases a path joins from the right and 100m further on the path forks. Keep left and in another 100m or so, as you enter a flat area of

Looking across Llyn Hywel to Y Llethr from Rhinog Fach

grass and heather (immediately below a broken vegetated rock slab separating the scree slopes above), the path swings right. Look for a narrow footpath on the left here which ascends a rocky depression in the slopes above (to the left of a large area of scree). The path is visible in its upper section but is more difficult to locate lower down.

Once you have located the path it is easy enough to follow. The upper section is steep but soon over. As the angle eases follow the path as it veers left, then right up to the north top. The walk to the main summit is now a delight—an easy undulating ridge with fine views on all sides.

From the summit take the path on the right-hand side of the wall that drops to the east. At a ladder stile turn right and soon you will be looking down on Llyn Hywel far below. Pass an upright rock and head diagonally-left down the broken slopes, scrambling over slabby ribs at one point to reach the wall again. Go right beside the wall crossing the top of the slabs which fall steeply into the lake.

As you begin the ascent to Y Llethr look back for the one of the finest and most famous views in the Rhinog—Rhinog Fach rising above Llyn Hywell.

The path rises more or less beside the wall then swings away right to zig-zag up the final rise to the flat summit. Follow the wall to the highest point marked by a tiny cairn,

In clear weather the view from any of the Rhinog hills is extensive and takes in the wide seep of Cardigan Bay, from the hills of the Lleyn Peninsula in the north to the curve of Pembrokeshire on the southern horizon. The mountains of northern Snowdonia can be seen in the distance with the bulk of Cadair Idris to the south across the Mawddach estuary.

From here follow the wall southwest down to the corner where there are two stiles. Cross the stile ahead and turn right following the wall along the broad ridge with the grassy dome of Moelfre ahead.

In about 2km/1 mile the wall turns right. Turn right with the wall and in about 200-300m go through a gateway in the wall. Ahead you will see a rough track beyond a stream (about 150m away) head for this and follow it left down to a farm. Don't go into the farm yard, instead turn left down the concrete access road to the lane. Turn right along the lane for about 2km/1 mile to return to Maes-y-garnedd.

Looking back to Rhinog Fach, Llyn Hywel and Rhinog Fawr from Y Llethr

Rhinog Fawr from just above Roman Steps

14. Rhinog Fawr from Cwm Bychan by Roman Steps

Outline: *Easy walking on an ancient stone paved trackway takes you into the heart of the Rhinog. From Bwlch Tyddiad a narrow path weaves between heather and rocks past the sheltered Llyn Du and up the mountain's northern slopes to the summit. Return is made by a more exploratory route through typical Rhinog terrain by Gloyw Llyn.*

Distance: *8.75km/5½ miles.*

Height gained: *667m/2,188ft.*

Summits: *Rhinog Fawr.*

Starting point: *Car park and campsite at the head of Cwm Bychan by the lake. A small fee is charged.*
Grid ref: SH 645 314.

ALTHOUGH THE MAJORITY OF WALKERS will have first become aware of the Rhinog hills from their striking outline seen from the east, often against a glorious sunset, there is little doubt that the best approach is from the west along the sinuous lane which leaves Llanbedr to rise beside the tumbling Afon Artro beneath a canopy of ancient oaks. At the head of the lane the sheltered Llyn Cwm Bychan comes as a pleasant surprise and at the same time a slight disappointment as the main summits fall out of view.

This route uses the famous Roman Steps to approach Rhinog Fawr, with a return by the beautiful Gloyw Lyn—a perfect finish on a golden evening.

The route: Go through the gate at the top of the car park and turn right onto the well-made path which crosses the stream and soon enters oak woods. After the woods, cross a small stone bridge and continue the ascent on the famous paved path known as 'Roman Steps'.

The steps—almost 500 in all—look recently laid and are of unknown date but almost certainly not Roman. This route through the hills is of great antiquity though and had probably been in use for several centuries before being paved. The steps are most likely of Medieval

origin and their purpose will quickly become apparent to anyone who wanders off-route.

Follow the path to the highest point of the pass (Bwlch Tyddiad) and continue ahead as it begins to descend toward the broad plantations which sprawl across the lower eastern slopes of the mountain. About 300m beyond the highest point, and immediately before a wall on the right which emerges from the heather and then swings away down the valley, bear right onto a narrow footpath which crosses the wall then rises between heather and rocks bringing you to the picturesque little lake of Llyn Du in its rocky hollow.

Follow the path along the right-hand shore scrambling over boulders to reach a well-built stone wall about 150m beyond the lake (note the

The view south from Rhinog Fawr to Rhinog Fach and Y Llethr

Gloyw Lyn with Rhinog Fawr in the background

stone stile in the wall here for possible descent). The path now heads left up beside the wall until the way is blocked by a small rock face. Turn right through a gap in the wall here and stay on the path which more or less follows the wall.

Stay with the path and the wall to reach a distinct level area carpeted in marshy grass just before the wall begins to descend. Immediately before this take the path left up the final rocky slopes of the mountain. A little higher where the path appears to level, bear right and make a final steep climb to the summit.

Here at the centre of the Rhinog the views are stunning in all directions—north across the rocky wilds of Moel Morwynion and Clip with the peaks of northern Snowdonia beyond, and south to Rhinog Fach, Y Llethr and Diffwys.

To return, retrace your steps down to the level marshy area by the wall. There are two main options from here. For the shortest route turn right and return to the stile in the wall by Llyn Du noted earlier. Go left over this and follow the visible path to cross a second wall. The path continues ahead eventually steepening to descend a shallow rocky gully with Gloyw Lyn visible below. Once on level ground go ahead over a large, grassy and sometimes marshy area to a point just before the southern end of the lake. Take the narrow path right here which passes high above the eastern shore following a rocky, slabby ridge. At the end of the lake a fisherman's path weaves down through the bracken and swings right to join the outgoing route below Roman Steps. Turn left to return to the car park.

Alternatively, for a slightly longer and more picturesque route go left at the level grassy area for about 200m or so. The wall is no longer visible but a narrow footpath on the right takes you back to it. Go through a gap in the wall and turn left beside it for about 100m to a point where it veers left. Take the vague path ahead (west) from here which soon swings rightwards (northwest) through the heather. At an obvious crossing path go left and follow it on a contouring line with Gloyw Lyn visible below.

Shortly the path passes above a wide gully on the right, its right-hand side composed of flat slabby rocks. At the bottom of the gully there is a stone wall crossed by a ladder stile. Shortly, the path swings right down to this stile. Cross the stile and follow the good path which heads left for a few metres before it swings right and then heads directly down towards Gloyw Lyn.

There are paths on either side of the lake but the left-hand option gives better views back towards Rhinog Fawr. At the end of the lake there are two fisherman's paths. From the left-hand side of the lake take the second path which heads down through the heather swinging rightwards to join the Roman Steps path near the little stone bridge. Turn left and follow the path back to the car park.

Arenig Fawr from the east

15. *Arenig Fawr & Moel Llyfnant by Llyn Arenig Fawr*

Outline: *A leisurely jaunt along a well-made track leads to a secluded, lonely mountain lake. This is followed by a moderate rounded ridge and an easy walk across the Arenig plateau with wide views. The south ridge of Arenig Fawr is then used to include Moel Llyfnant with a return by forest roads and lanes.*

Distance: *16.25km/10 miles.*

Height gained: *920m/3,315ft.*

Summits: *Arenig Fawr & Moel Llyfnant.*

Starting point: *There is a small layby on the old lane from Bala through Llidiardau to Arenig where a track leads up to Llyn Arenig Fawr. You can reach this point from the A4212 west of Llyn Celyn but the Llidiardau approach gives excellent views of the mountain to whet your appetite. Grid ref: SH 845 395.*

ARENIG FAWR DOMINATES THE WILD EMPTY MOORS TO THE west of Bala. Standing head and shoulders above its neighbours, Moel Llyfnant and Arenig Fach, and separated from anything of similar height, it reigns supreme. Usually seen from the north where it presents a rather uninviting quarry-scarred bulk rising above the southern shore of Llyn Celyn, the mountain is completely different when seen from other angles—the bulky lower slopes adding presence to its twin pointed summits.

This route includes both Arenig Fawr and its near neighbour Moel Llyfnant. The two can not be combined without substantial height loss and a long return via forest roads and lanes, but the effort is well worth it giving a walk with superb views and a rare feeling of remoteness.

The route: Cross the stile by the gate and head off up the track which takes you quickly and with minimum effort to Llyn Arenig Fawr, cradled in a sombre hollow below the blocky eastern face of the mountain.

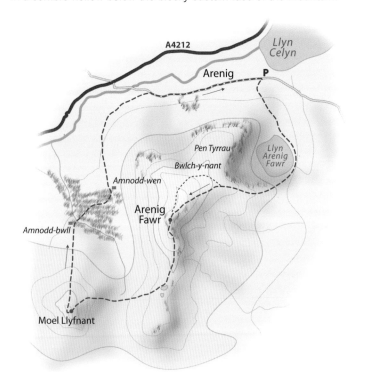

Llyn Arenig Fawr with Llyn Celyn in the distance

The lake is contained by a small dam and the track ends by a tiny disused sluice house now converted to a refuge. A good footpath passes the hut to ford the stream close to the outflow from the dam, then swings away through the heather up the rounded steepening ridge beyond.

This requires the first real effort of the ascent but height is gained quickly and at a second fence the angle eases and the summit comes into view. The path bears right here over the fence to a small boggy level area (Bwlch-y-nant) before curving left across the grassy eastern flanks of the mountain below the crest of the ridge. The path follows a gently rising traverse line at first before rising more steeply through an area of broken rocks to reach the broad summit plateau a few hundred meters northeast of the triangulation pillar.

The isolated location of this summit with no near neighbours gives a rare feeling of wildness. The view north takes in the broad expanse of the Migneint and Hiraethog moors, with the Clwydian Range on skyline. East lie the Berwyns and the Aran ridge with the more striking outlines of Cadair Idris to the south. To the west, the serrated skyline of the Rhinog hills dominate the western panorama, with the giants of northern Snowdonia away to the northwest.

If you do not want to extend your walk beyond Arenig Fawr the options for a circular route are limited. It is possible to follow the northwest ridge and make a direct descent to join the path along the valley north of the ruined farmstead Amnodd-wen, but this is steep, trackless and involves a section along the lane. Probably the best option is to return via Llyn Arenig Fawr. This maintains the interest of the ascent as well as easing tired legs. It is however, worth the short out-and-back detour to the south top before striking out northeast following the remains of the old fence across the plateau rather than the final section of the ascent. Where the fence divides at GR. 829 373 continue northeast over gentle undulating ground. At the end of the ridge lies an area of flat slabby rocks and small pools (Pen Tyrrau). As the ground steepens before you reach this bear right to join the ascent route at the level boggy area (Bwlch-y-nant). Retrace the ascent route from here.

To continue the walk to Moel Llyfnant, head south along the ridge over the south summit and on down the broadening south ridge where the rock soon gives way to grass. There are faint paths developing but nothing you could reliably follow in the mist, the fence being the best guide in poor visibility.

Looking back to the summit of Arenig Fawr from the south ridge

CADAIR IDRIS IS THE BEST KNOWN AND GRANDEST MOUNTAIN in southern Snowdonia. Its complex of ridges and deep crag-lined cwms has more in common with the giants of the north, yet here it is overlooking the rolling hills of mid Wales.

Its most striking feature is the great north-facing escarpment which rises dramatically above the Mawddach estuary, but it is hard to devise a satisfactory circular walk of reasonable distance on this side of the mountain. This southern approach circles the impressive hidden amphitheatre containing Llyn Cau with stunning views all the way.

The route: Go through the gate at the back of the car park by the information board and turn right along an avenue of trees. Cross the bridge and soon pass in front of the 'Ystradlyn Visitor Centre'. After the footbridge turn right through a gate into the nature reserve to begin the stiff pull up through woods beside the tumbling river over to the right.

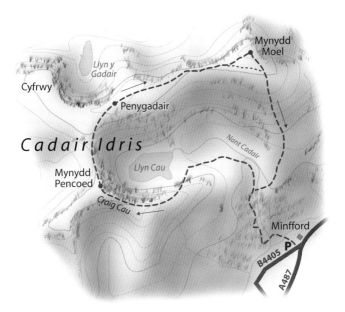

Nearing the summit of Mynydd Moel, Panygadair behind

As you emerge from the woods the path bends left towards the enclosed lake of Llyn Cau which remains out of view until you are almost at the water's edge.

On the lip of the cwm the path splits—the path ahead leads down to the shore of the lake with the path to the left rising up towards the ridge. It is worth the short detour to the edge of the lake for the stunning view of Craig Cau towering above the dark water, but you will need to return to this junction to continue.

As you gain the ridge you are treated to fine views southwards across the Tarren hills and beyond. Bear right along the edge of Craig Cau to the subsidiary top of Mynydd Pencoed perched on the very edge of the huge cliffs overhanging the lake (take care in poor visibility!).

From Mynydd Pencoed make a short descent due north to the saddle separating it from Penygadair, Cadair's highest point. From here a short stiff pull takes you onto the summit.

In clear conditions the view out over the Mawddach estuary and across Cardigan Bay to the hills of the Lleyn Peninsula is magnificent, particularly late in the day with the promise of a fine sunset. With reasonable clarity the entire curve of Cardigan Bay should be visible from Bardsey (Ynys Enlli) to the tip of Pembrokeshire. Inland to the north lie the Rhinog hills with the mountains of northern Snowdonia on the horizon. Nearer at hand to the northeast and east lie the Arenigs and Arans, while to the south the rolling hills of mid Wales disappear beyond moors of Plynlimon.

From the summit head east across the broad summit plateau following the edge of the cliffs on the left towards Mynydd Moel the next top, just over 1km/½ mile away. As the ground begins the gentle rise to Mynydd Moel either continue to the summit, or take the contouring path which breaks away right. Eventually a wall is either reached or is visible down to the right. Head for this and descend steeply on its left-hand side. From Mynydd Moel reach the wall by a direct descent south-southeast.

Follow the wall to a stile (in about 1km/½ mile) on the right. Cross the wall here and head down rightwards to cross the stream (Nant Cadair) by a footbridge near the point where the Minffordd Path (used earlier) emerges from the woods. Turn left and retrace the outward route down through the woods beside the stream back to the car park.

Craig Cau and Mynydd Pencoed
rising above Llyn Cau

Aran Fawddwy and Aran Benllyn from Drysgol

17. *Aran Fawddwy & Aran Benllyn from Cwm Cywarch*

Outline: *From the impressive head of Cwm Cywarch a steady climb takes you onto the rounded shoulder of the mountain where a sweeping grass ridge leads onto the rocky summit plateau. Almost level out-and-back walking allows you to bag all three high summits before a damp return over moors to the foot of Craig Cywarch.*

Distance: *17km/10½ miles.*

Height gained: *1086m/3,560ft.*

Summits: *Aran Fawddwy, Aran Benllyn & Gwaun y Llwyni.*

Start: *There is free parking available on a large stretch of open common land near the head of Cwm Cywarch.*
Grid ref: SH 853 185.

OFTEN OVERLOOKED IN FAVOUR OF THEIR MORE FAMOUS NEIGHBOUR, Cadair Idris, the Aran hills remain unjustifiably neglected. Even the impressive sight of Aran Benllyn rising at the head of Bala Lake seems to entice few to venture into these hills.

This route approaches the two highest summits from Cwm Cywarch where the towering castellated buttresses of Craig Cywarch present one of the most impressive sights in southern Snowdonia. It is remarkable that this area is so little visited.

The route: From the parking area continue along the lane towards the farms at the valley head and in about 300m turn right over a footbridge signed 'Aran Benllyn and Aran Fawddwy'. The path is enclosed by walls at first, then rises diagonally up the open slopes of Pen yr Allt Uchaf, with impressive views back to Craig Cywarch.

Where the angle eases on the broad flat shoulder of the mountain, bear left up the rounded grass ridge parallel to the fence. Cross a stile

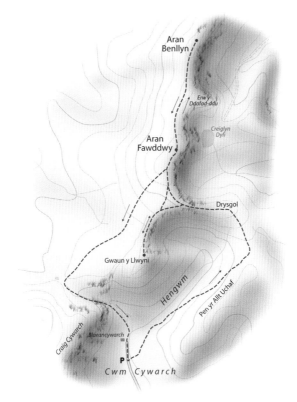

on the skyline at the top of the rise (Drysgol) and walk along the gentle grass ridge with good views right to the craggy eastern face of the two Aran giants. At the memorial cairn there are equally impressive views back down the sweeping Hengwm towards Craig Cywarch.

(Gwaun y Llwyni, seen so impressively from Hengwm, can be included by an out-and-back walk southwest along the ridge from here.)

The path heads northwest now along the edge of the cwm to cross a stile below the final rocky slopes of the mountain. A faint path leads through the jumbled boulders to a sub top at GR. 860 221. From here it is a short amble northeast across the stoney plateau—reminiscent of the Glyderau—to Aran Fawddwy. For peak baggers it is another 1.5km/1 mile to Aran Benllyn, a good option in clear weather for its superb views north across Bala Lake (Llyn Tegid).

From Aran Fawddwy return to the sup top, then head southwest to cross a stile in the fence ahead (ignore a stile on the right). Follow the footpath beside the fence which becomes better established as you descend. Things get pretty wet in parts but board walks take you over the worst sections.

Looking north from Aran Fawddwy along the ridge to Erw y Ddafad-ddu and Aran Benllyn with Bala Lake in the distance

Looking back to Craig Cywarch from the shoulder of Drysgol

Continue to the lowest point on the moors ahead before the ground rears up to the bulky mass of Glasgwm (just over 3km/2 miles from Aran Fawddwy). There is a small reedy pool here almost on the watershed. Turn left on a footpath which soon follows the stream down beside the towering crags of Craig Cywarch.

In about 1.5km/1 mile, join a track near a small cottage over to the left ('Bryn Hafod') and go right passing a farm ('Blaencywarch') to join the lane. Follow the lane back to the parking area to complete the route.

Mara Books & Northern Eye Books

www.marabooks.co.uk or www.northerneyebooks.com

Mara Books publish a range of walking books for Cheshire and North Wales and have the following list to date. A complete list of current titles is available on our web site.

North Wales
Mountain walking
Mountain & Hill Walking in Snowdonia

This is a two-volume in-depth guide to every summit of note in the Snowdonia National Park.

Volume 1 – Carneddau, Glyderau, Snowdon and Eifionydd. ISBN 978 1 902512 18 1.

Volume 2 – Moelwynion, Rhinogydd, Arenig, Arans, Dyfi hills and Cadair Idris as well as the Tarrens and Berwyns. ISBN 978 1 902512 22 8.

A Pocket guide to Snowdon

ISBN 978 1 902512 16 7. A guide to all Snowdon's recognised routes of ascent, from the six 'Classic Paths' to the many lesser known and less frequented routes.

Leisure walking
Coastal Walks around Anglesey

ISBN 978 1 902512 20 4. A collection of circular walks which explore the varied scenery of Anglesey's beautiful coastline, designated an Area of Outstanding Natural Beauty.

The Isle of Anglesey Coastal Path – The Official Guide

ISBN 978 1 902512 13 6. A guide to the 125-mile circuit of Anglesey's stunning coast, an Area of Outstanding Natural Beauty.

Walking in the Conwy Valley

ISBN 978 0 9522409 7 6. A collection of circular walks exploring the varied scenery of this beautiful valley from the Great Orme to Betws-y-coed.

Walks on the Lleyn Peninsula
ISBN 978 1 902512 00 6. A collection of circular walks which explore both the wild and beautiful coastline and hills of the Lleyn Peninsula.

Walking in the Clwydian Range
ISBN 978 1 902512 14 3. A collection of 21 circular walks in the Clwydian Range Area of Outstanding Natural Beauty.

Walking in the Vale of Clwyd and Hiraethog
ISBN 978 0 9559625 3 0. A collection of circular walks exploring the undiscovered country between the Clwydian Range and the Conwy Valley.

Walking in Snowdonia *Volume 1*
ISBN 978 1 902512 06 8. Twenty circular walks exploring the beautiful and dramatic valleys in the northern half of the Snowdonia National Park.

Mountaineering

The Mountain Men
ISBN 978 1 902512 11 2. This book tells the story of the pioneer rock climbers in Snowdonia in the closing decades of the nineteenth century until the outbreak of World War I.

The Day the Rope Broke
ISBN 978-1-902512-12-9. The story of the first ascent of the Matterhorn by the Victorian mountaineer Edward Whymper and the disaster which followed. Illustrated in colour and black and white.

Some common Welsh place name elements found in Snowdonia and their meaning:

Afon *(a-von)* .... river
Allt *(al-th-t)* .... slope
Bedd *(beth)* .... grave
Bwlch *(bul-k)* .... pass
Bychan *(buc-an)* .... small
Clogwyn .... crag/cliff
Crib/Gribin .... ridge
Cwm *(coom)* .... glacial valley
Ddu/Du *(thee, dee)* .... black
Ddysgl *(this-gul)* .... dish
Dyffryn .... valley
Fach/Bach *(vach)* .... small
Fawr/Mawr *(vaw-r)* .... large
Glas .... green, blue
Goch .... red
Graig/Craig .... crag
Gwastad .... plain, level
Llan .... church
Moel *(moy-l)* .... bald or rounded hill
Mynydd *(mun-uth)* .... mountain
Nant .... stream
Pen .... head
Rhyd .... ford
Saethau .... to shoot, arrows
Wen, gwyn .... white